MASTERING THE
OBVIOUS
A Handbook for Home, Work, and School

A Simple Approach to a Better Life

- **Improve** your quality of life.
- **Enjoy** greater productivity.
- **Increase** your profitability.

Based on Principles of the *Work/Life System*
Developed by

RICHARD C. GILLESPIE
Master of the Obvious

MASTERING THE
OBVIOUS
A Handbook for Home, Work, and School

A simplified approach based on work/life principles that
were created to help improve the human condition—quality,
productivity, and profitability—at work, school, and home

RICHARD C. GILLESPIE

author of *Managing Is Everybody's Business*
and coauthor of *A Practical Approach to
Performance Interventions and Analysis*

Archway Publishing books may be ordered
through booksellers or by contacting:

Archway Publishing
1663 Liberty Drive
Bloomington, IN 47403
www.archwaypublishing.com
1 (888) 242-5904

ISBN: 978-1-4808-2402-7 (sc)
ISBN: 978-1-4808-2403-4 (e)

Library of Congress Control Number: 2015918185

Print information available on the last page.

Archway Publishing rev. date: 11/3/2015

CONTENTS

Setting the Stage vii

CHAPTER 1   Useful Information................................. 1

CHAPTER 2   Telling and Persuading v. Asking
and Sharing... 7

CHAPTER 3   1–20 Thinking Out Loud.......................11

CHAPTER 4   Understanding, Acceptance, and
Support (UAS) 19

CHAPTER 5   Arc of Distortion 27

CHAPTER 6   What I Permit I Promote.......................31

CHAPTER 7   Valuing Behavior 39

CHAPTER 8   SEA Problem Solving and
Opportunity Analysis.............................45

CHAPTER 9   Organizational Bill of Rights..................55

CHAPTER 10   Strategic and Operational Managing......59

About the Author 63

Acknowledgments 65

SETTING THE STAGE

All people have their own social, political, economic, and religious beliefs; they also are of different races, genders, and ages. I respect these differing views and circumstances; however, this book reflects my eighty-three-plus years of experience. Over fifty of these years are directly related to promoting organizational and individual quality of work and life at home and on the job.

During these years I continued to pursue my personal avocation of studying Christian theology. A primary focus for me was the work of St. Augustine because I wanted to understand why Martin Luther was an Augustinian monk.

St. Augustine, who is generally the most recognized theologian (after St. Paul) of the Bible, was a prolific

writer and is still being studied by people who understand the critical need to see our world as a theocracy—
meaning that the god of the Holy Bible is in charge of
our world!

St. Augustine was born in AD 357 and died in AD 430.
What has this to do with this book?

He was constantly asked to write a short summary of his
most critical ideas for lay people to understand. His book
is called the *Enchiridion* (en-krid-e-on). Many people
today are not aware of the *Enchiridion* and go through
their lives without the benefit of this useful information.

This caused me to realize that I needed to write a hand-
book simplifying the complexities of my two previous
books. With that said, I ask for your patience as you consider these ideas for your best advantage. Use those that
fit your needs and ignore those that don't. Thank you!

I have shared the following simple work/life ideas with
thousands of people over the past fifty years. These
ideas are contained within the Work/Life Approach, a

complex organizational development model. The Work/ Life Approach is dedicated to providing a practical means for helping individuals, families, and organizations become more competent in using their knowledge, skills, and experience for improving their private and public quality of life.

I have received comments from people that these simple ideas are just common sense, yet those same people lack the *common sense* to use them.

I attribute the failure to use these ideas to the most difficult human behavior to disguise: *arrogance.*

Arrogance gets in the way of the most difficult human behavior to maintain: humility. Humility requires persistence, intensity, and consistency.

- Persistence because the natural tendency of people is to believe they don't need humility.

- Intensity because humility takes constant personal focus to do what is right.

- Consistency because true humility is experienced both in our beliefs and our actions.

About fifty years ago I was made aware of a concept called the *indispensable man*. It was described to me this way: Fill a bucket up with water, and then reach your arm down to the bottom and pull it out quickly. If there is a hole left in the bucket, then you are indispensable.

I've not found anyone able to leave a hole in the bucket; however, I have found numerous people who act like they are indispensable.

My intent is to humbly share these ideas with you. You are the judge whether I succeed or not.

By the way, I'm constantly fending off arrogance myself. I keep working on improving my batting average to personally eliminate my arrogant behavior.

These concepts are published in two books. The first book, *Managing Is Everybody's Business,* was published in 1992 and is currently out of print.

The second book, *A Practical Approach to Performance Interventions and Analysis,* was coauthored with Dr. Gene Fusch in 2012 and is available on Amazon.com.

These two books are of immense value to those who are willing to study them and focus on the complex challenges of personal and organizational change.

Others prefer a shorter version for quicker reference to facilitate integration into their current personal and organizational working beliefs. This book is the shorter version.

CHAPTER 1

Useful Information

In order to be useful, information needs to be relevant, valid, timely, and reliable.

If information doesn't fit the situation, it is not relevant and therefore is not useful.

If information is not accurate and doesn't convey what it means to convey, it is not valid and therefore is not useful.

If information is too late or too early, it isn't timely and therefore is not useful.

If the source of the information (human or other) is not reliable, it can't be trusted and therefore is not useful.

All four of these elements must be met for information to be useful.

For over thirty years, I have introduced this definition to many private, public, and educational organizations including many individuals. In all these years everyone confirms this idea as critical, and yet few integrate it into their daily conversations.

Why? Because people would have to be more careful about what they say.

People have been put down for being truthful.

People withhold useful information for their own benefit. People take little time to find out what is really happening because after all, there is little time to do it right, but always time to do it over.

These are just a few reasons for starters. I'm sure you could come up with many more.

Think about it—what a poor work or home life to live!

Useful information is:

- *Relevant:* fits the situation.

- *Valid:* conveys what it means to convey; it is accurate and meaningful.

- *Timely:* is not too soon and not too late.

- *Reliable:* the source, human or other, is trusted.

Useful information is vital.

- The most prevalent form of organizational theft is the withholding of useful information.

- Focus on the work.

- When we share useful information, we help people do the work they were hired to do.

NOTES:

CHAPTER 2

Telling and Persuading v. Asking and Sharing

Once again, arrogance shows up here. It could come from the owner, supervisor, know-it-all associate, family member, friend, professional "expert"—you could make up your own list.

Telling and persuading is a universal way of insulting other people. It lacks the opportunity to gain the opinions of others and conveys the know-it-all approach. It could also justify the idea that time is of the essence and the opinion of others is not worthy. In some cases, it comes across as "my mind is made up; don't confuse me with the facts."

Stop and think of all the hard feelings, wasted time, loss of good ideas, and financial waste due to this approach when being inconsiderate of other people. It is a matter of choice.

Asking and sharing rely on humility. Humility recognizes the worth of ideas from others, seeks to understand differences, and promotes buy-in. It can take more time up front, with a more valuable end result and increased cooperation in the future.

Asking and sharing is one of the vital concepts for persistently increasing trust and the quality of life at home and work.

- Telling and persuading

    – Gets resistance

- Asking and sharing

    – Gets ownership

NOTES:

_____

_____

_____

_____

_____

_____

_____

_____

_____

_____

CHAPTER 3

1–20 Thinking Out Loud

I was recently listening to a person who sees the possibility of a change in his current job. The person wanted to express some ideas, yet held them back because the people in charge had not established a working environment fostering ideas from associates without them being asked.

This is a prime example of fostering the withholding of useful information, caused by fear of rejection and possibly not being given the time to thoroughly present the ideas.

Ideas don't care who have them; only that they get used.

Withholding ideas costs time, money, and reduction in mutual trust (even more than the actual stealing of money and other assets).

How many people do you know that were fired for with-holding useful information?

How about those supervisors who prevented people from sharing useful information?

The 1–20 Thinking Out Loud concept provides every-one the opportunity to *share* their ideas in a nonthreat-ening environment. Here is how it works.

If I come up with a wild idea that has very little due dil-igence behind it, I introduce the idea with these words: "I have a wild idea, and I am only at a 1."

That is a one on the scale of 1–20, with 20 meaning thoroughly developed. This gives me a chance to at least start some thinking with others who have a stake in the situation without their jumping to the conclusion that I am already at commitment (20). I am freed up to invite them to participate and ensure mutual acceptance to accept or reject the idea. *Everyone gets heard!*

Another way to use this concept starts with an associate being given an assignment. At this point both the supervisor and associate are at a 1. When the associate comes back to the supervisor with the completed staff work on the assignment, the associate is at a 20, meaning a commitment to the work being presented to the supervisor. During the feedback session, the supervisor may have additional questions that cause the associate to move back to 12, requiring the need to gain more useful information before the assignment is complete.

The intent of the 1–20 concept is for people regardless of their position in the organization to share ideas without intimidation, valuing the opportunity to interact about the work while knowing that there is no such thing as a dumb idea or that a person's title automatically makes the idea better.

The 1–20 concept is an invaluable model to use at home and in social situations. Children can use it with their parents to test out the possibility for getting permission to go somewhere or to do something currently not clear.

Couples can use it to negotiate differences of opinion and seek mutual buy-in for making significant decisions.

This concept frees up people who have broad executive and managerial authority to speak up about ideas, with an open opportunity for others to interact equally.

For example, the owner may start with, "I have a wild idea, and I am only at a 7 on the 1–20 scale."

- Verbal self-talk

    - Wild idea shared immediately

    - Above the line

- Nonverbal self-talk

  - Idea held and then shared; almost to commitment

  - Below the line

- Above or below the line

  - Either is okay

- 1–20 scale

NOTES:

_____

_____

_____

_____

_____

_____

_____

_____

_____

_____

CHAPTER 4

Understanding, Acceptance, and Support (UAS)

Time is always at a premium. When a situation occurs that requires attention, the tendency is to skip a thorough analysis, which includes seeking useful information from others who should be involved.

Many times the end result is costly, creates ill feelings, and fails to be the correct solution. Following the UAS concept eliminates this exposure.

Let's look at each element separately.

Understanding

We have all been to the medical doctor and experienced probing throughout our bodies until the doctor is satisfied that all aspects have been checked out so that the situation is clear before moving on to a diagnosis.

During the probing process, questions are asked, and unique equipment is used to determine the facts. Simultaneously there are ongoing activities and questions relating to feelings. Feelings are legitimate, and actions must be responsible. While this is occurring, there is constant information explaining why all this needs to be done, which explains the motive for these activities.

This same process is necessary in all aspects of both work and homelife. Unfortunately most people lack the willingness to thoroughly *understand* what is going on before they jump to conclusions that best suit their arrogant opinions, desires, needs, and so on.

To offset this arrogant behavior, it is necessary to deal with acceptance.

Acceptance

This is where *humility* enters into the picture.

People deserve to have an opportunity to be heard! In the heat of the battle, it takes a lot of patience to listen to people's whole story.

To gain acceptance there must be an operating climate of *trust*, openness to stay focused on the situation, and a checking out whether people are sharing wild Ideas or if they are already at commitment.

The previously noted 1–20 concept provides a great opportunity to seek to understand where there are misunderstandings. It discloses the need to listen more carefully to substantiate commitment.

In many situations there is the necessity to accept the final decision even when there is not full commitment. Acceptance does not mean agreement. There are times to remember that groups don't make decisions.

Support

Support acknowledges that people have been heard and willingly leave, committed to fulfill their obligations. Anyone who leaves and does hallway weeping (not buying into the decision and griping about it to others after the meeting is over) is insubordinate and deserves to be fired!

Gaining UAS is one of the most important concepts to work at as a means to increase the habit of operating with *humility*.

- Understanding

  - Probe for clarity

  - Check out facts and feelings

  - Be up-front about motives

- Acceptance

  - Being heard

  - 1–20 scale

  - Does not mean agreement

- Support

  - Commitment to the results

NOTES:

_____

_____

_____

_____

_____

_____

_____

_____

_____

_____

CHAPTER 5

Arc of Distortion

The key to reducing the *arc of distortion* is to recognize that all of us are responsible for making sure that we have clearly articulated the message we have sent and clearly listened to the message we have received. To do this we need to use the UAS concept with the understanding that we are not perfect at either sending or receiving messages.

Keep in mind that each of us have our own values, habits, beliefs, knowledge, skill, experience, and understanding as we interpret what useful information is being sent or received.

I have noticed that during meetings people have a tendency to carry on side conversations, *utilize electronic devices*, and interrupt the speaker before the speaker has completed a thought. This is impolite, as well as a major cause for increasing the *arc of distortion*.

There are times when it is important to take notes as an aid to ensure clear UAS and reduce the *arc of distortion*.

- Meanings are in people, not in words.

- The sender takes responsibility for sending—UAS.

- The receiver takes responsibility for receiving—UAS.

- To reduce the arc of distortion, seek to understand and seek to be understood.

NOTES:

CHAPTER 6

What I Permit I Promote

Pristine is one of the signature facets of a restaurant that strives to be the best in its class. What does *pristine* mean?

The best description is to consider the requirements for having a clean emergency operating room in a hospital. The same is true for all aspects of a restaurant.

How is this accomplished in a restaurant? It starts with a clear UAS that *pristine* is a condition for employment!

When management permits anything less, they are promoting substandard work. For example, if floors have spots on them and are not cleaned up, it is a given that other substandard aspects of the work in the restaurant are also being ignored.

What I *permit* sets the stage for success or failure. There is no way for half measures to achieve *excellence*.

What I promote means setting a standard and adhering to it. Setting an example for excellence means doing what is expected with a sense of:

- Persistence, meaning there is no excuse for failing to do it right the first time!

- Insistence, following what is expected, when it is expected, and why it is expected!

- Consistency, meeting the UAS end results!

The consequences for compromising *pristine* are obvious.

Ignoring the obligation to implement consequences *permits* continuing substandard end results.

- What I *permit* I *promote.*

- The easy things are *easy* to do.

- The easy things are just as easy *not* to do.

NOTES:

The wisest men that e're you ken

Have never deemed it treason,

To rest a bit—and jest a bit,

And balance up their reason;

To laugh a bit—and chaff a bit,

And joke a bit in season.

CHAPTER 7

Valuing Behavior

Valuing behavior integrates *work behavior,* *work attitude*, *useful information*, and *effectiveness*.

Work behavior can be defined as the visible and audio expressions individuals and combinations of individuals reflect as they implement their UAS commitments to accomplish the work.

Some behave *negatively most of the time*, and that is *de-valuing behavior*! They tend to find fault, pin blame, ignore the need to change, interrupt others, use vulgar language, do sloppy work, withhold useful information, fail to see value in others, lie, cheat, steal, have poor hygiene, *and a whole lot more actions* that drag down the working climate wherever they are—at home, in public, or on the job.

Devaluing behavior is a major cause for *distrust* and directly affects both physical and intellectual degeneration.

Some behave in *positive ways most of the time*, and that is *valuing behavior*! They tend to respect others, focus on their work, give credit when credit is due, and seek to understand and be understood. They willingly help others and tend to give more than they get. They are patient, will forgive others and forget past mistakes by them, and demonstrate a loving and caring presence.

The basis for *devaluing behavior* is generally an attitude of distrust and fear and cannot be seen! It is the foundation for behavior that is visible.

The basis for *valuing behavior* is an attitude of trust and generic love. Remember, *attitude is not seen; it is reflected by behavior.*

Useful information is withheld due to devaluing behavior.

The more people are valued, the more willing they are to share useful information, which increases trust.

Trust is increased by valuing behavior and sharing useful information.

None of us is perfect. I'm often asked, "How are you doing?" My answer is *"Next to perfect. My wife is perfect, and I'm next to her." I'm luckier than most.*

Effectiveness is directly related to *trust*!

This means all people who work at valuing behavior and sharing useful information automatically increase overall effectiveness. To quote Tevye in *Fiddler on the Roof*: "It isn't easy."

NOTES:

CHAPTER 8

SEA Problem Solving and Opportunity Analysis

Stop and think for a moment! The past doesn't exist, and the future doesn't exist. Life is lived moment by moment.

That is why the idea that the world is a *theocracy* is so important. God of the Bible has known and knows everything past, present, and future; he is present everywhere and is all-powerful. Many people have not, do not, and will not believe this! Those of you who do not believe this have already wasted your precious time reading what I have written so far.

This chapter promotes the idea that every moment is situational. This means that we are always aware of *what is happening and what is going on.* The question is always "To what extent do those we live, work, and associate with UAS the same end result?" The first activity in both problem solving and opportunity analysis is to take time to find out.

You will find that all the previous chapters contain ideas that integrate with the situation. For example, if *useful information isn't UAS*, it is another waste of time to go on.

The second activity is to determine either "what should be happening or going on" or "what could be happening or going on," and gain UAS.

The third activity is to determine if there are any *differences* or *deviations* between the first and second activities. If either of these exists, then a problem or opportunity exists.

The fourth activity is to determine cause or causes if there is a problem and gain UAS. If there is an opportunity, then before going on, gain UAS for the desired end result.

The fifth activity is to take time to validate that the expectation for the "should" or "could" is still legitimate.

The sixth activity is to develop ways to handle the problem or ways to develop the opportunity. In both cases consider multiple *alternatives*. Remember, a decision is a choice or choices of alternatives.

The seventh activity is to implement *action*!

This process is for all situations! There are times when it takes only minutes to implement and times when it takes hours, days, even years to implement.

Why do people avoid using this Situation-Expectation-Action (SEA) discipline for their personal well-being?

One of the most significant human disciplines is to tighten people's feeling valve and open their thinking valve. This provides an opportunity to focus on the facts and integrate feelings as they become useful information.

How important is it to always share useful information during every waking moment of each day as *we* struggle to solve problems and create new opportunities?

What is it going to take to have schools provide this gift to children from junior high on? Think of the difference it could make for their opportunities to be magnified because they are competent in problem solving and decision making.

What if the workplace made these ideas a condition for employment? It would be a gift to the workers' families for them to take home ideas that enhance their quality of life. *It would be a free gift from their employer. Want to put a dollar value on that?*

The question is "*What is the alternative* if this Situation-Expectation-Action (SEA) discipline is not used?" For some, there is "Never time to do it right; plenty of time to do it over." For others—businesses fail, people lose their jobs, the workplace is devaluing, families break up, and public entities waste time and money and create misery.

Stop and *think*! Make up your own list and search for your contribution. Are you making life better for those around you or not?

The dilemma is that people use ideas that meet their selfish interest. There are no universal consequences for failing to adopt these ideas. We are at war with our arrogant sense of pride whether we know it or not. I'm thankful for being blessed with the strength to do daily battle, having put on the full armor of God of the Bible.

It would take hundreds of pages for me to give you examples of the value of this information. My examples are private to the situation. Create your own experiences.

There are five types of action to consider depending on the situation:

- Adaptive

  - Live with it.

- Interim

  - Meanwhile; until we get it solved

- Preventive

  - Strategic future; prevent, anticipate, and block

- Corrective

  - Do something different.

- Contingent

    - If, make preparation, potential for, subject
      to the situation

NOTES:

CHAPTER 9

Organizational Bill of Rights

My first job out of high school in 1950 was to join the US Air Force. The Korean "conflict" had just started in May 1950, and I knew I would be quickly drafted. I mention this because I was committed to do the job for which I was being paid $75 a month. Fifty dollars was automatically sent to my savings account back home.

Every month we would line up in the recreational room, where a table was set up with piles of greenbacks—cash to you younger folks.

I never felt that I had to back up to that table to receive my $25. I knew I earned it. Some of the airmen should have had to back up to receive their pay because they sloughed off from doing their work.

It takes integrity to give more than you get. I have always strived to do this!

This chapter deals with the *work itself*!

When a person accepts a job, it is important to document specifically the scope of the work, the individual's required knowledge, skills, and experience, and the desired end results. This combined information helps to define the value and potential for growth and development on the job.

Money is not a motivator! It is recognition for the value of the work and the individual's performance.

People need to understand

- What they are hired to do.

- The results expected from them.

- How they will know when their work is done.

- The knowledge, experience, and skills required.

- The resources (financial, physical, and time) required.

People also need

- regular feedback and to

- share in rewards.

Integrity

Consider the following numeric model for providing people with specific useful information that leaves no misunderstanding regarding their UAS performance.

1–2	3–4	5–8	9–10	11–12
poor performance	below standard performance	standard performance	above standard performance	outstanding performance

Motivation comes from visualizing the future with a means to accomplish the desired end results. Meaningful work is the responsibility of supervisors to sincerely articulate the interdependence of all work that spells success for the enterprise.

People deserve to receive consistent feedback regarding their contribution to the success of the enterprise.

They also deserve to be paid what the value of the job is worth. Every job should have a predetermined range, which should be clearly explained to individuals before they are hired.

CHAPTER 10

Strategic and Operational Managing

Methods

Tempus Fugit

Measurement

The strategic and operational models noted below were developed while I was working with the John L. Scott management team. They provide a simple road map for strategic and operational flow of work.

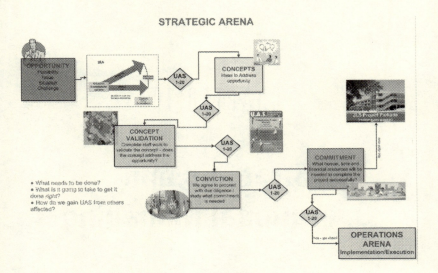

Strategic arena

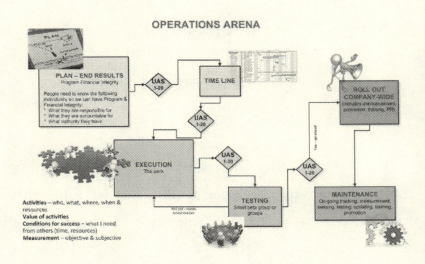

Operations arena

These concepts—for the strategic arena and for the operations arena—have separately proven their value for improving the human condition, productivity, quality, and profitability in both public and private endeavors as well as homelife, regardless of race, color, creed, or age. They are all *working beliefs*!

ABOUT THE AUTHOR

Richard C. Gillespie helps organizations realize their desired end results with leadership audits, change management initiatives, and financial turnarounds.

Gillespie is referred to as the Master of the Obvious because of his ability to provide a succinct and straightforward work/life approach to resolve complex business, public, and human services needs.

Some of his clients have included Lutheran schools, colleges, and universities, the US Forest Service, Weyerhaeuser, John L. Scott Real Estate, B&B steel fabricators, Red Robin, and Salty's restaurants.

In addition to consulting, Gillespie has served as president of Dri-Eaz Products and chief operations officer for Salty's Seafood Restaurants.

ACKNOWLEDGMENTS

Special thanks to Kathy and Gerry Kingen, owners of Salty's Seafood Restaurants, as well as their general managers and executive staff; Lennox Scott, owner of John L. Scott Real Estate, for his twenty-plus years of integrating these ideas in his business; and Dan Youra, who published my first book and provided technical assistance on this one.

Thank you most of all to my wife for her patience and support.

"Dick, how are you feeling?"

"I'm next to perfect. My wife is perfect, and I'm next to her!"